Huffing & Puffing
Harnessing the Power of Story

Sal Lucido

Huffing & Puffing

First Printing: 2016

ISBN 978-1-365-30811-6

Visit us for more content at: www.bizpoapp.com

Email me your feedback at: info@mod.rent

Morgan Hill, California 95037

Once Upon A Time...

"If there is a magic in story writing, and I am convinced there is, no one has ever been able to reduce it to a recipe that can be passed from one person to another."

— John Steinbeck

Can Storytelling be Taught?

John Steinbeck believed that there is no recipe for passing story writing magic from one person to another. I disagree - this book is my story writing recipe. This is good news because story writing and storytelling is a big part of what makes us human.

"The human species thinks in metaphors and learns through stories."

-Mary Catherine Bateson

The purpose of this book is to enhance your inner storyteller. And while this book's lessons can be applied to any type of story, it is specifically aimed at vision-sharing stories. If you haven't delivered a vision-sharing story yet, you've most certainly been on the receiving end of one. Vision-sharing stories are all around us. They take the form of business presentations, startup pitches, web video talks, podcasts and speeches. These stories are used to inform, enlighten, garner enthusiasm, and recruit resources.

Every great human accomplishment started off as an idea inside someone's head. But before these ideas become reality, they are communicated as stories. Prior to spanning the San Francisco Bay, the Golden Gate Bridge was just a story. Prior to uniting the world's athletes in peaceful competition, the dream of the Olympic Games existed as merely a story. Before a man walked on the moon, U.S. President John F. Kennedy said,

> *"Many years ago, the great British explorer George Mallory was asked why he wanted to climb Mount Everest. He said because it's there. Well space is there, and we're going to climb it."*

Instead of telling you what to do, this book focuses on what to avoid. Through understanding and avoiding these most commonly made storytelling mistakes, you can quickly and easily improve the stories you tell. And since most of us learn best by example, this book is centered on one very familiar, surprisingly well-constructed tale – the story of *The Three Little Pigs*. So before we get to the top-ten storytelling mistakes, allow me to present to you Joseph Jacob's version of *The Three Little Pigs*…

(NOTE: Even though most of us have already heard this story – it is important that you read Jacobs' version from beginning to end before moving on to the next chapter.)

The Three Little Pigs

Joseph Jacob

English Fairy Tales, 1890

THERE was an old sow with three little pigs, and as she had not enough to keep them, she sent them out to seek their fortune.

The first that went off met a man with a bundle of straw, and said to him, "Please, man, give me that straw to build a house." which the man did, and the little pig built a house with it.

Presently came along a wolf, and knocked at the door, and said, "Little pig, little pig, let me come in."

To which the pig answered, "No, no, not by the hair of my chiny chin chin."

The wolf then answered to that, "Then I'll huff, and I'll puff, and I'll blow your house in." So he huffed, and he puffed, and he blew his house in, and ate up the little pig.

The second little pig met a man with a bundle of sticks and said, "Please, man, give me those sticks to build a house." which the man did, and the pig built his house.

Then along came the wolf, and said, "Little pig, little pig, let me come in."

"No, no, not by the hair of my chiny chin chin."

"Then I'll huff, and I'll puff, and I'll blow your house in." So he huffed, and he puffed, and he puffed, and he huffed, and at last he blew the house down, and he ate up the little pig.

The third little pig met a man with a load of bricks, and said, "Please, man, give me those bricks to build a house with." So the man gave him the bricks, and he built his house with them.

So the wolf came, as he did to the other little pigs, and said, "Little pig, little pig, let me come in."

"No, no, not by the hair of my chiny chin chin."

"Then I'll huff, and I'll puff, and I'll blow your house in."

Well, he huffed, and he puffed, and he huffed and he puffed, and he puffed and huffed; but he could not get the house down. When he found that he could not, the wolf was very angry indeed, and declared he would eat up the little pig, and that he would get down the chimney after him.

When the little pig saw what he was about, he hung on the pot full of water, and made up a blazing fire, and, just as the wolf was coming down, took off the cover, and in fell the wolf; so the little pig put on the cover again in an instant, boiled him up, and ate him for supper, and lived happy ever afterwards.

0

Let's stop huffing and puffing - and start telling impactful, memorable stories.

Introduction

You have just read one of the earliest publications of *The Three Little Pigs* by Joseph Jacobs. As arguably the best-known version of the story, it appeared in Jacobs' book titled *English Fairy Tales*, published in 1890. Why has this story survived the ages? You probably recognize this version of the story even though it was published a century ago. It appears to be a fairly simplistic story, and upon cursory reading it seems largely unremarkable. Yet this tale occupies a spot in our 21st century conscious. And surprisingly, a nearly identical version of this story is still told today. Why? What is it about this story that makes it so enduring? What lessons can we learn about storytelling from this tale? This book explores these questions and presents a list of *ten storytelling mistakes* we need to avoid when telling our own stories. It also illustrates how Jacob's was able to avoid these mistakes to construct his masterfully written, enduring story. And at the end of this book I provide you with a storytelling scorecard that can be used to grade and improve the stories you tell and the stories you hear.

Huffing and Puffing is the title of this book, and huffing and puffing is what we want to avoid. We've all been victims of boring business presentations, uninspiring startup pitches, long-winded, confusing web videos and speeches. The aim of this book is to deliver us from this fate, so let's jump right into the first storytelling mistake...

"I've learned that people will forget what you said, people will forget what you did, but people will never forget how you made them feel."

- Maya Angelou

Story Telling Mistake #1: No Emotion

Even though *The Three Little Pigs* is a children's story, it arouses strong emotions. It makes you feel something. The pigs face real danger and two of them meet their demise...

"So he huffed, and he puffed, and he blew his house in, and ate up the little pig."

As the story progresses we get angrier and angrier at the wolf. And by the end of the story we are very happy to hear...

" ...so the little pig put on the cover again in an instant, boiled him up, and ate him for supper."

Way to go third little pig! Connecting on an emotional level is an essential element of good storytelling and Jacobs does exactly that. The characters are in mortal danger. The story evokes fear, hope, and celebration in victory. Unfortunately, most storytelling and vision sharing is absent of emotion. This is especially true when it comes to business proposals and startup pitches. The heavy emphasis on facts and figures leaves little room for the human element of vision sharing. This is a grave mistake. Most great ideas are not easily implemented. And the thing that carries us through the hard times is emotional fortitude. So when we leave out the emotions, we build what I call a

Tin Man Story - a story without heart. A vision without heart is doomed to failure.

So which emotions should we elicit? How can we connect with our audience on an emotional level? What is the proper balance between emotion and information? These are important questions, so let's take them one at a time.

What do we want our audience to feel? How do we go about deciding which emotions we need to evoke? We do this by examining our own motivations. What does the story mean to us personally? Why pursue this dream? Why tell this story? It is very difficult, if not impossible, to fake our emotions. So the best way to authentically move our listeners is to speak from the heart. I recommend that you start by listing out all of the reasons why you are motivated to tell the story. What drives you? How do you feel about the subject? What would be lost if the vision doesn't become a reality? Once you have a comprehensive list of the reasons why you are passionate about the story, it will be time to road test them. Present them to your family, your close friends and colleagues. Test the connecting power of each motivation; each emotion. Not all of them will resonate. You will find that some of your motivations connect better than others. Rank them, and craft your story around the one or two motivations you feel resonate best with you and your listener. This will ensure that your story connects on both an emotional and on a personal level.

Note that there will always be deep, personal reasons for telling a story or accomplishing a dream, and they are all important. However, "higher callings" resonate more broadly than "self-serving motivations". I am sure that President John F. Kennedy had personal reasons for setting the moonshot goal. Who knows, maybe he thought it would be exciting to go into outer space or hold a moon rock. Certainly, having a man land on the moon during his presidency would have added to his legacy. Yet, despite any personal motivations he may have had, his speech is centered on more universally held aspirations.

> "...space is there, and we are going to climb it... and new hopes for knowledge and peace are there."

Once you've decided on your story's emotional focus, you are ready to weave it into your tale. So, what is the best way to accomplish this? Well, I like to open my presentations with a statement that speaks to the heart. Then I like to follow this up with my intellectual arguments. And then I like to finish with a heartfelt conclusion. This 'storytelling sandwich', comprised of facts bookended by two pieces of heartfelt bread - is a very effective combination. Jacobs uses the same structure in *The Three Little Pigs*. His first sentence describes the mother's hope for a prosperous future for her children. And while the meat of the story-sandwich is concerned with the life events of her offspring, the last sentence in the story assures us that the third pig lives happily ever afterwards.

So now that you've added some heart to your story, let's take a look at the second storytelling mistake...

2

"There was an old sow with three little pigs, and as she had not enough to keep them, she sent them out to seek their fortune."

Story Telling Mistake #2: Confusing

In the story of *The Three Little Pigs*, a mother sends her three children out to seek their fortune and their life choices dictate whether they live or die. Jacob's story is very straightforward. It is easy to understand. Every action logically leads to the next. The relationships between the characters are uncomplicated; mother, children, predator, and prey. The story goes down easy because it's both relatable and understandable. It doesn't require extra knowledge. We can learn from Jacobs and set this as the bar for our stories.

We have all observed how a skilled person can make a difficult task look easy. As we've already noted, Jacobs' version of *The Three Little Pigs* appears simplistic and unremarkable on the face of it. However, crafting such a 'clean story' is not as easy as it looks. Ideas as they exist in our mind seem so straightforward and obvious. Then as we attempt to express these ideas something goes wrong. The story gets complicated, and confusing. Our listeners don't get what we are trying to say. They get lost. They have questions. Why is it so difficult to clearly and concisely convey an idea? How can we be more like Jacobs and tell a straightforward, understandable story? Well, luckily there are some techniques used by Jacobs that we can emulate.

The first technique involves the power of the journey. By nature we humans are explorers and exploration requires travel. What's around the bend? What's over that hill? And since exploration is built into our DNA, the human brain is designed to comprehend stories of expedition. *The Three Little Pigs* is told in this manner. It is told as a journey. The children are sent out to fend for themselves. They meet people, barter for goods, and build their homes. Each event leads

9

logically to the next. The motivations make sense. A mother cannot provide so she sends her children to seek their fortune. The children leave home and are now in need of new homes. We are on the journey with the pigs and follow along with anticipation for what will happen next. So let's learn from Jacobs. We can reduce confusion by framing our stories as journeys.

But if our story is not a physical journey, how can we frame it as such? The answer is to follow the journey format. Each point should logically lead to the next point. Each assertion should be queued up as a dilemma posed by an earlier assertion. When we describe a dilemma, the audience waits with anticipation for what will resolve it. A journey goes somewhere. It has a first step. It has a destination. A journey involves obstacles that need to be overcome. Even if our story is not a physical journey it can have these attributes. The best stories paint a picture of the destination. Listeners want to reach the promise land. And the more real it seems, the more willing the audience will be to take the trip. Let's face it – we all want to live *happily ever after*.

So, besides framing our stories as journeys, what other techniques employed by Jacobs can we use to reduce confusion? Well, one thing Jacobs does very well is that he keeps the relationships between the story elements uncomplicated. The character relationships are straightforward. There is a mother, her children and a villain. There are no second cousins or third uncles once removed. And while Jacobs' technique may seem obvious, most of us are guilty of violating this principle. So we need to examine our story elements and eliminate superfluous relationships. We need to make our stories easier to understand and kick out all of the second cousins and first uncles once removed.

The final technique employed by Jacobs for keeping the story uncomplicated is that he doesn't require the listener to acquire special knowledge. While the premise of talking pigs with carpentry skills is not something any of us have encountered in our daily lives, the rest of the story is familiar. It doesn't require us to learn something we don't already know. We need to follow this example. We can do this by limiting the amount of new knowledge required by our listeners. It is difficult enough to convey an idea without burdening it with unfamiliar concepts. We shouldn't complicate matters by including uncommon knowledge. As demonstrated by Jacobs, common knowledge is the best setting for our stories.

So in summary, we need to use Jacobs' techniques for keeping our stories uncomplicated. We should frame them as journeys, simplify the relationships between the story elements, and limit the amount of new knowledge required by our audience members. All of these edits will not only improve our stories, they will also help us to avoid this next storytelling mistake...

3

"The more you leave out, the more you highlight what you leave in."
— Henry Green

Story Telling Mistake #3: Too Long

The entire *Three Little Pigs* story, while fully formed, can be told in a matter of minutes. Having been passed down from generation to generation, this story had time to evolve into the concise tale we know so well. I believe the story was purposefully distilled down to its current form so that it could be recited as a bedtime story. And prior to the advent of radio and television, this was probably an essential tool used by tired parents trying to get rambunctious children to go to sleep at night. Our vision sharing stories should undergo this same distillation process.

Undisciplined bedtimes get later and later, and undisciplined stories grow longer and longer. Why? There are many reasons. Over zealousness can turn stories into never-ending diatribes. Underestimating our audience's IQ can result in over explaining. I find that a great way to get control over length is to create three versions of the story. I recommend creating a short version, a medium version and a normal version of your story. The 'normal version' of your story should take about fifteen minutes to present. The medium version of your story should only take a couple of minutes to tell. And the short version of your story should only be one sentence long. The benefit of this exercise is that it not only helps you trim the length of your main story, but each version serves a useful purpose as well. So let's take a look at each of these versions and discuss how they can be used.

Let's start with the short version of your story, which will boil your entire tale down to one, well-constructed sentence. You are likely already familiar with this as it is commonly referred to in the business world as an *elevator pitch*. In the movie business this is know as a *logline*. As the 'business world' name implies, this version of the story should be able to be recited in the time it takes one to ride an elevator. The purpose of the elevator pitch or logline is two fold. It should not only convey a synopsis of the story, it should also provide the emotional hook that gets your listener to ask for more information about the idea. Let's take a look at some real-world examples:

Here is the elevator pitch for the homestay company *Airbnb*.

Book rooms with locals rather than hotels.

Here is the logline for the movie *ET*.

A troubled child summons the courage to help a friendly alien escape Earth and return to his home-world.

Notice how both of these one-sentence "stories" contain enough information to convey the idea being proposed while at the same time piquing your curiosity about the idea. The 'short version' of your story should do the same thing. Creating this version of your story forces you to strip it down to its core purpose. A successful single sentence story has your listener nodding with understanding and then asking you for more. And this is where the 'medium version' of your story comes into play.

The medium version of your story should only take a couple of minutes to tell. In essence it should be one paragraph long. This version should be long enough to get into more detail, answer some high level questions and yet short enough to recited in one or two minutes time. If this version of the story takes much longer than this to tell, then most people will tune out. The purpose of this version of the story is to answer the tip-of-the-tongue questions prompted by the short version and to entice your listener to formally meet and discuss the guts of your idea. This is where the 'normal length' version of your story comes into play.

The normal length version of your story is your formal 'pitch'. In the business world the 'pitch' is usually presented in a formal, sit-down setting, and is accompanied by visuals and or handouts. It should be able to be presented ideally in 15 minutes, which fits comfortably into a typical 45 minute meeting where most of the time is dedicated to setting up, introductions, waiting for late attendees to arrive and finished off with a healthy question and answer period.

So avoid Storytelling Mistake #3 by authoring three versions of your story. I believe that if you had to pick only one of these ten mistakes to avoid, this would be my top choice. Authoring these three versions will force you to create a story that avoids most of the other storytelling mistakes. As you work on these versions, keep in mind this next storytelling mistake, because the best way to spread an idea is to have it retold by others.

4

"I'll huff and I'll puff and I'll blow your house in."
"No, no, not by the hair of my chiny chin chin."

Story Telling Mistake #4: Not Memorable (Forgettable)

This lyrical refrain and its variations are repeated three times in Jacobs' story.

"I'll huff and I'll puff and I'll blow your house in."
"No, no, not by the hair of my chiny chin chin."

It's not only something you 'can' memorize, it's something you 'want to' memorize. And beyond being catchy, it's original. Whoever came up with this concept of blowing down a house with huffs and puffs is a genius. There are many ways a predator might break into a house. Maybe the predator would knock down the door, or claw through the walls. But huffing and puffing? Who thought that up? I know that I wouldn't choose this breaking-and-entering methodology. Yet, these are the nuances that make the story so special, so memorable, so retold. If you want your story to be passed along (and you do!), craft it so that people **can** retell it and more importantly, **want to** retell it! If you only take one thing away from this book make it this…

If our listeners enjoy our story they will be more inclined to tell it to someone else.

Understanding this one concept is the key to successful storytelling. If our listeners like our story; if they like our idea enough to take action on it they will have to justify themselves to someone else. This means they will have to retell the story! So it's our job to arm them for this task. Construct your story so that your listeners can retell it to someone else. This someone else might be a friend, a significant other, or a business associate. If you craft your story so that it is easy to retell, you increase the odds that your ideas will live on.

"I'll huff and I'll puff and I'll blow your house in."

"No, no, not by the hair of my chiny chin chin."

How can we craft our stories so that they have a high probability of being retold and like the story of *The Three Little Pigs*, live on? First of all, heed the advice of the story telling mistakes we've already discussed regarding emotions, understanding and length. And then learn from Jacobs - stand out, become sticky, focus, and repeat. Because demolition by huffing is so unexpected, it stands out. Because huffing and puffing and chiny chin chin are so lyrical, they are sticky. Also, repeating this refrain three times make it almost impossible to forget. So how do we employ these techniques?

At the 2016 North American Leaders' Summit, held in Ottawa, Canada, US President Barack Obama, Canadian Prime Minister Justin Trudeau and Mexican Prime Minister Peña Nieto each gave a closing speech. And while these speeches were well written and skillfully delivered, only one thing was memorable for me - the monarch butterfly. Prime Minister Nieto said this about the Monarch Butterfly, which migrates each year from Canada through the United States to Mexico...

"Finally, I would like to use an example to describe our level of integration. The preservation of the monarch butterfly conservation — this is a species that, in its pilgrimage, we can see how our countries are intertwined. And back in our last summit, we agreed that we would take care of this species and make sure that in its journey, the

monarch butterfly from Canada, flying through the United States all the way down to Mexico. And by that, we will be making sure the migration of this species is the symbol of the relationship that Canada, the United States and Mexico has. Isolationism is not the solution. In contrast with what happens in other corners in the world, the countries in North America, we have decided to be closer, to work as a team and to complement each other and to make progress together as the most competitive region in the world."

I remembered nothing from these three professionally crafted speeches, except, of course, Nieto's butterfly. It stood out. It was different. And best of all, it was on point. The plight of the butterfly illuminates and encapsulates the challenges discussed at the North American Leaders' Summit. Finding a memorable, on-topic way to convey your point is not easy to do, but it's well worth the effort. And if you manage to find a standout storytelling strategy, don't forget to make it sticky, focus and repeat.

Let's talk briefly about stickiness. The master of stickiness was the attorney Johnny Cochran, made famous by the OJ trial. You can probably guess what quote I'm going to use as the stickiness example.

"If it doesn't fit, you must acquit."

This one, rhyming, lyrical line not only summed up the case for Cochrane's jury, it was hyper memorable. You not only 'could' repeat it, you 'wanted to' repeat it. I imagine that some of the jurors even repeated it as a rational for finding OJ not guilty when deliberating the verdict. Now, you don't need to include a poetic refrain in your stories to make them memorable, although it doesn't hurt, but you do need to give your listener something they can repeat. Why climb Mount Everest? Why go to space? Most people having heard the line before are able to answer these questions...

Again, crafting a hyper sticky refrain is not easy to do, but well worth the effort. But even if you succeed in standing out and getting sticky, you can still ruin all your good works with what I call - clutter. So how do we keep ourselves from cluttering up our stories? Focus and repeat. As the shampoo bottle instructions so famously state...

"Lather, rinse, repeat."

In order to keep from cluttering our stories so that they will be memorable and retold, we must lather, rinse and repeat. Focus on one main point and repeat it throughout the presentation. Use the work you've already done in the three previous storytelling mistake exercises to narrow in on the one emotionally connecting, understandable, concise point you want to make. Then construct your story dutifully around that singular, powerful idea. Do not clutter it with anything else. Keep it clean. Let it stand. Make it stand out. Make it sticky. Trust your main point. Trust your butterfly.

Let's finish by discussing the idea of repetition. Flatly repeating the same thing multiple times is not advisable. It is tedious, unsophisticated and ultimately ineffective. As a master storyteller, Jacobs was not only aware of this fact, he knew the antidote - the rule of three. In writing, it is understood that things grouped in threes are more satisfying, funnier and more interesting. And because of these attributes, the listeners are more likely to remember the information. Imagine the story of Goldilocks and the Two Bears, or worse yet, the Four Bears. The best way to stir repetition into your story is to come at your theme in three similar but interestingly different ways. You don't want all your bears to be the same age and gender. You don't want all your pigs to build brick houses. So if you want your stories to be memorable and retold (and you do), select a single, powerful theme, convey it in a way that stands out, keep your story focused and uncluttered and use the rule of three to add interesting repetition. And then in order to make sure all of your hard work doesn't go to waste - avoid this next storytelling mistake...

5

"As she had not enough to keep them, she sent them out to seek their fortune."

Story Telling Mistake #5: Weak Start

From the very first sentence of Jacob's story, we are hooked. She had not enough to keep them. This implies the mother wanted to keep them but she had not enough. As a parent we relate to this problem. As a child we certainly wouldn't want to see our parent put in this situation. As a child we wouldn't want to be in this situation, suddenly sent out to seek our fortune. From the very first sentence of Jacobs' story we are engaged. We feel for the mom. We are pulling for the pigs. Jacobs knew that it is essential for a story to have a strong start. We only have a few seconds at the beginning of our stories to grab our audience. We need to ensure that the first sentence has impact. In order to avoid this storytelling mistake, craft the beginning of your story so that it grabs your audience.

So how do we create a strong start? Well it's not easy. In fact there is a tongue-in-cheek literary contest based solely on this challenge. The *Bulwer-Lytton Fiction Contest* is a whimsical literature competition sponsored by the English Department of San Jose State University. Entrants are challenged to compose the opening sentence to the worst of all possible novels. And while we are trying to learn how to not create our 'worst' story, the contest still requires contestants to hook the audience in the space of one sentence. The creativity of these contestants is incredible.

This is the entry from the 2016 winner:

> *"Even from the hall, the overpowering stench told me the dingy caramel glow in his office would be from a ten-thousand-cigarette layer of nicotine baked on a naked bulb hanging from a frayed wire in the center of a likely cracked and water-stained ceiling, but I was broke, he was cheap, and I had to find her."*
>
> — *William "Barry" Brockett, Tallahassee, FL*

From this single sentence, we are hooked. What has driven this person to spend what little money he or she has to find this mystery woman? Who is she? Where is she? The *Bulwer-Lytton Fiction Contest* winning entries are great examples for how a single opening sentence, written correctly, is enough to spark the imagination. Your story's opening sentence has the power to do the same thing. Your opening sentence can spark the imagination of your listener. So how can you accomplish this task of hooking the audience with one sentence? You do this by making sure the opening sentence contains these three ingredients: emotion, vision and challenge.

> *"Four score and seven years ago our fathers brought forth on this continent, a new nation, conceived in Liberty, and dedicated to the proposition that all men are created equal."*

Abraham Lincoln's Gettysburg Address was delivered to a young America on the verge of splitting in two. In his opening sentence he reminds his listeners of the founding fathers' original vision as a challenge for the nation to remain united. Emotion, vision and challenge. If your opening sentence includes these three elements, it has a good shot at engaging your audience.

Now before we jump into the next storytelling mistake let's talk about a story's finish. While Jacobs opted for the 'happily-ever-afterwards' ending, it is also important to finish strong. Strong finishes are remembered. Weak finishes fade. Professional comedians understand this dynamic, which is why they always save their best joke for last. Moviemakers also know about this technique. This is the reason that some add 'out takes' to the closing credits of their movie. A strong finish can save even the worst movie.

So how do we go from a weak finish to a strong finish? Think give-and-take. What do you want your listener to give and what do you want them to take away. At the very least we want our audience to give us their attention and feedback. Sometimes we want the audience to give resources in the form of funding or effort. Determine what you need the audience to contribute and clearly state how they can accomplish the task at the end of your story. If the purpose of your story is to recruit volunteers, make sure you ask for this service and describe exactly how it can be exercised. Clearly state the call to action, concisely and clearly at the end of the story.

In addition to the call to action, the ending should clearly state the primary takeaway of your story. Unfortunately the audience will not remember most of what was said in the story. Therefore, it is important to clearly state what you want the audience to remember at the end of the story. This is your final chance to make a lasting impression, so it is important to boil the takeaway down to one, clearly stated point. Your story's finish leaves an aftertaste. Make sure this aftertaste is exactly what you want it to be. Remember, your story's finish is a give-and-take.

6

"The first that went off met a man with a bundle of straw."

Story Telling Mistake #6: Too Much

There are three men in Jacobs' story with building supplies needed by the pigs. Who were these men? What were they doing with these goods? Why would they give away straw, sticks and bricks just for the asking? These are all very good questions. But Jacobs does not address them at all in the story. Why? He does not go into these details because they are not essential to the plot. The story stands without them. Jacobs understands that in order for this tale to have maximum impact and to ensure that it could easily be retold, some seemingly crucial plot points would have to be eliminated. I can't emphasis this next statement enough ...

Remove everything that is not absolutely essential to your story.

The most important and most difficult thing you need to do when crafting your story is to decide what not to say. Learn from Jacobs and be absolutely loyal to telling one and only one story.

If you've every read a book that has been turned into a movie you understand this concept. Since movies do not have enough time to mirror the book, editing takes place, and seemingly crucial parts of the book are omitted from the movie version of the story. And while fans of the book tend to be outraged by these omissions, those that haven't read the book are perfectly content with the movie's storyline.

This type of editing is a skill and discipline that every great storyteller must master. The challenge is that, as an author, it is difficult to omit things. Everything seems absolutely essential. But it has to be done. Focused stories are able to create an immediate and lasting impact. Meandering, rambling stories are confusing and quickly forgotten. Remember, the ultimate compliment is having your story retold by others. A succinct, impactful and memorable story stands the best chance of being retold.

So how do you go about deciding which plot points to omit from your vision-sharing stories? The first five storytelling mistake exercises have removed some of the fat. Now you need to remove some of the muscle. This sometimes requires you to experiment with versions of the story that omit seemingly crucial arguments and plot points to assess the effectiveness of various versions of the story. If your listeners are confused, and ask you about what was omitted, then you may need to reinsert the point. However, if your listeners are perfectly content without knowing about what was omitted, then leave the content out. No matter how interesting or exciting the omitted items are, you are better off without them. Remember, the wellbeing of your audience is more important than your own, which brings us to the next storytelling mistake...

7

The Big Bad Wolf

Story Telling Mistake #7: Condescending

What's the purpose of *The Three Little Pigs* story? What makes it worthy of being retold? Is there some wisdom, some lesson being passed down from generation to generation? It is considered a fable after all. Let me ask you this. Take a guess at how many times Jacobs refers to the pig's adversary as the big bad wolf.

Imagine Jeopardy music playing now while you consider your answer….

If you guessed a number larger than zero, you guessed wrong. Jacobs never once refers to the adversary as the big bad wolf. Jacobs tells the story without judgment.

"Storytelling reveals meaning without committing the error of defining it."

-Hannah Arendt

Jacobs never tells us what to think or how to react. Why? Because master storytellers let the story do the talking. They understand that the audience should be left alone to interpret and judge these things for themselves. The story is crafted in a way that is respectful of the listener's intelligence. It gives the reader room to draw their own unique conclusions. To do otherwise is disrespectful and condescending to the audience. So follow Jacob's example and never, no matter how tempting, tell your audience what to think. Let your vision stand on its own merits. Be respectful of your listener, not condescending.

Having heard my fair share of sales presentations and startup pitches, I have been told what to think more times than I care to remember…

> Presenter: "This is hands-down the greatest product ever!"
>
> Likely Reaction: "Yeah? Well I'll be the judge of that."
>
> Presenter: "This business can't miss, everyone will want to be our customer and no one has what we have!"
>
> Likely Reaction: "Really? I don't want to be your customer and I know of three companies that have that."

By telling the listener what to think, we are not only being condescending, we are setting ourselves up for failure. When a listener is told what to think, their natural reaction is to challenge the assertion. This assertion-challenge exchange is what I role-played above. And as you can see - this isn't a back-and-forth we want to be having with our audience. When selling the moonshot project, imagine if JFK had said we should do this because it's the greatest idea ever. I am sure it was tempting for Jacobs and JFK to let their personal enthusiasm and judgments be known, but as master storytellers they knew better.

Let the story speak for itself and give the listener room to draw their own conclusions. Eliminate hyperbole and opinion from your story. This discipline will elevate you to the rank of master storyteller, setting you apart from the crowd. And when you're done sweeping away the opinions and assertions, keep your broom handy for this next storytelling mistake.

"Please, man, give me that straw to build a house." Which the man did, and the little pig built a house with it.

Presently came along a wolf, and knocked at the door, "Little pig, little pig, let me come in."

Story Telling Mistake #8: Sloppy

In the excerpt above, Jacobs introduces a man and describes some sort of transaction involving straw. He subsequently let's us know that the pig constructs a house with said straw, and introduces us to the pig's first visitor. Jacobs tells us that this visitor is a wolf, who proceeds to knock on the pig's door to request entrance into the pig's house. Jacobs does all of this in three succinct sentences. The entire story is skillfully crafted in this compact fashion. Read the story again and notice how succinctly the tale is told. This is not by accident. Jacobs carefully managed the length and pace of his story. If we want our stories to have maximum impact in a minimal amount of time, we must purposefully construct each sentence to rapidly and efficiently convey our ideas. Sloppiness is the enemy of great storytelling.

Great storytelling feels conversational and spontaneous while in reality it is carefully crafted and diligently choreographed. One way to achieve this is to read your story out loud to someone. An impactful vision-sharing story with staying power should be able to be presented verbatim, live to an audience. A sloppy, awkwardly written meandering story will fall flat with a live audience. Conversely, an understandable, fast-moving story keeps an audience riveted and entertained.

You know you have removed the sloppiness when the written words work as a spoken presentation. This is how books found on the bestsellers list are authored. As you read them, you can hear the author's voice in your head. Even though each sentence is meticulously crafted, they feel spontaneous, natural and conversational. This is the balance you are looking to strike. Sloppy storytelling is cumbersome and forgettable, while, carefully crafted and practiced storytelling is enjoyable and memorable. Now that you've carefully crafted a succinct, impactful story, it's time examine your story's veracity.

9

Build an accurate, honest, believable base from which your listeners can take their leap of faith.

Story Telling Mistake #9: Not Believable

On the face of it, a story about talking pigs that know how to build houses seems a bit far-fetched. Yet Jacobs tells the story in a way that makes it believable. This is the same challenge we face with our own vision-sharing stories. We are tasked with explaining how pie-in-the-sky ideas can become reality. Land a man on the moon? No problem - we can do it. Build a bridge across the San Francisco bay? Cake! So what's the secret to getting our audience to believe? Balance. Every vision-sharing story needs to strike a balance between fact and faith. Dreams require belief in something that does not yet exist. But the road to that dream must be paved with realistic cobbles. If you succeed in striking this balance, your audience will take the journey with you. If not, then your journey to a better place will be a lonely one.

One of the surest ways to loose believability is to misrepresent the facts. If your story is found to be inaccurate, if it states wrong dates or incorrect statistics, then everything in the story looses credibility. Make sure the premise for your vision is solid. Fact-check everything that can be verified. Build an accurate, honest, believable base from which your listeners can take their leap of faith. This will keep your audience buckled up for the ride.

Next, make sure your story is self-consistent. Jacobs story does require some suspension of reality but it is self-consistent. Even though pigs don't talk, their motivations and actions ring true. The story is logical from an action-consequence point of view. A mother cannot provide for her children and they are sent out to fend for themselves. Follow Jacob's lead and make sure each assertion logically follows from the previous.

The other thing to keep in mind pertaining to believability is the mantra 'less is more'. This is a central theme for most of these storytelling mistakes. By streamlining and focusing your story, you make it more understandable, more memorable and – yes, more believable. Every assertion and plot point is run through the listener's *believability checker*. By streamlining and focusing your story, you lower the odds of tripping up. I've seen many a presentation derailed by a questionable assertion that was not central to the story. And backtracking and explaining a spurious point not central to the story is something you want to avoid at all costs.

Now before we get into the *Storytelling Scorecard*, which is a great tool for grading the stories we hear and tell, let's discuss one final storytelling mistake that we might assume Jacobs did not make...

In order to find the good in the bad, you can't take criticism personally.

Story Telling Mistake #10: No Outside Input

If by chance you took it upon yourself to find and read Jacobs' version of the *Three Little Pigs* you would have discovered an edit. I have purposefully omitted part of the story. Near the end of the tale, the wolf unsuccessfully tries to trick the third little pig into leaving his house of brick. I made this edit for two reasons. I wanted to show an example of an extremely compact story so I trimmed it down. And I wanted to give you permission to seek and implement outside help. No story, even Joseph Jacobs', is perfect. Every story can and should be continuously improved. Therefore, we must always be open and receptive to outside inputs.

Now, not all inputs will come in the form of constructive criticism. Some feedback is outright insensitive and hurtful. Nevertheless, you have to check your ego at the door and be receptive to the information. Sometimes the best advice is dressed in super villain clothing. In order to find the good in the bad, you can't take criticism personally. You must temporarily disconnect yourself from your creation in order to view it from the listener's perspective. And by being receptive as opposed to defensive, you not only position yourself to learn something important, you increase the odds of winning over initially skeptical listeners. Sometimes your harshest critics become your most passionate fans.

There is another thing you can do to garner listener feedback. You can employ a testing strategy. A majority of audience members will not provide honest feedback. In an effort to avoid confrontation, most listeners just smile, nod and mumble mild approval. In order to actively obtain feedback website developers employ what's called A/B Testing. They create an A and B version of a webpage and randomly display them to website visitors. They then monitor the conversion rate for each version to test effectiveness. Based on the data, they then keep the superior version and discard the inferior version. And they don't stop there. They then add yet another version to test against the superior version. This test and improve process is repeated until the website meets its conversion rate goals. If you like, you can implement this type of testing by authoring two versions of your story and testing the effectiveness of each by gaging audience reactions. Keep the superior version and experiment with a new test version. This type of testing can sometimes yield surprising results and lead you in a new and unexpected direction.

Conclusions

By eliminating these ten storytelling mistakes, your stories will have a stronger impact and greater staying power.

Storytelling Scorecard

We've finished exploring ten common storytelling mistakes. We've examined how Joseph Jacobs was able to craft the story of *The Three Little Pigs* into the treasure that we recognize it to be today. Whether or not he knew it, Jacobs was successfully able to avoid making these mistakes. And I believe that is why his story has survived to this day. The premise of this book is that we can learn from Jacobs. When we think about adding emotion to our stories, we can reflect on the mother pig's plight and her hope for a bright future for her children. When we struggle with the task of streamlining our narratives, we rest assured that a simpler, more focused story is a better story. And if we want our stories to survive and be retold, we can emulate the succinctness and catchiness of Jacobs' tale, knowing that his version has stood the test of time.

As promised, I have included a *Storytelling Scorecard* at the end of this book. Use it to evaluate the stories you hear and the stories you tell. Stories matter. Storytelling is a uniquely human endeavor. Our dreams start out as stories. Therefore, the better our stories are, the more likely our dreams are to come true. Keep on dreaming. And keep on storytelling.

"Every great dream begins with a dreamer. Always remember, you have within you the strength, the patience, and the passion to reach for the stars to change the world."
- Harriet Tubman

STORY TELLING SCORECARD

Check off the mistakes made and refer to the applicable chapter for guidance on how to improve the story.

o **No Emotion:** Do I care? Was I emotionally moved or connected to the story? If no then refer to Chapter 1.

o **Confusing:** Do I fully and readily understand the story? If no then refer to Chapter 2.

o **Too long:** Was the story delivered in a timely manner? If no then refer to Chapter 3.

o **Not Memorable:** Could I easily retell the story and convey its key point to someone else? If no then refer to Chapter 4.

o **Weak Start and Stop:** Did the opening hook me? Was the ending impactful? If no then refer to Chapter 5.

o **Too Much:** Did the story go into irrelevant or extraneous topics? If yes then refer to Chapter 6.

o **Condescending:** Did the presenter explain the obvious or come across as didactic? If yes then refer to Chapter 7.

o **Sloppy:** Did the presentation feel haphazard or come off as rambling? If yes then refer to Chapter 8.

o **Not Believable:** Is the story unbelievable? Is there too much hype? If yes then refer to Chapter 9.

o **No Outside Input:** Was the author receptive to outside input? If no then refer to Chapter 10.

❖ Visit our website for more content: www.bizpoapp.com

❖ Email me your feedback at: info@mod.rent

www.ingramcontent.com/pod-product-compliance
Lightning Source LLC
Chambersburg PA
CBHW021852170526
45157CB00006B/2412